Believe in Me, for I Am the Way

Richard DeGiacomo

Editing and typesetting: Sally Hanan of Inksnatcher.com
Cover design: German Creative

Believe in Me, for I Am the Way/Richard DeGiacomo
ISBN 9798671130171

To Elaine, who is always there for me.

Table of Contents

Preface

The world today is in a state of chaos. It is a planet of wars, pandemics, civil unrest, soaring crime rate, and a moral decline in the advancement of civilization. Our own great country is experiencing an unraveling of what this republic stands for, namely, freedom, opportunity, equality, and justice for all.

There is a political divide that in my lifetime has never been experienced. Differences of opinions are healthy and should be discussed, but the political divide over the past years has grown from a difference of opinion to individual hatred. There is civil unrest throughout this country, and many others, resulting in rioting, looting, and even death. Is that what we are all about? No, it is not. If corrective measures do not take place, I believe that this republic will self-destruct. It is the opinion of some historians that it was Abraham Lincoln who so eloquently stated, "the only way this nation will be destroyed is from within." It is disturbing to say, but it appears we might be headed in that direction.

I believe the only way we can get our republic back is through a relationship with God. May this book help you find your way to Him.

Richard

1

Does God Exist?

The only proof for the existence of God is that
without God, you couldn't prove anything.
—*Cornelius VanTil, philosopher*

Unfortunately, many in our country of 350 million do not accept or believe in the Word of God. They have no understanding of who He is, or why He should be believed if He does exist. I pray that those who are not believers will realize, before it is too late, the importance of having God in their lives. He is our Creator, the Creator of this world and of all that is or ever will be.

Before forming a negative opinion of Christianity, do some research. You owe it to yourself to be sure of what you accept or reject.

Creation

What we do know and believe is attained through faith and the Word of God, as stated in the Holy Bible. God is a divine Being and our Creator. He is the Creator of all that is, ever was, and ever will be. In other words, He is the Creator of everything. If God did not exist, we never would have been created and, therefore, there would be no salvation. There would be no planet earth or any planets or universes. There would be nothing. That is not a pleasant thought.

Do you know of anyone who can create something out of nothing? The answer can only be no. If you can accept that fact, then you have already answered the question of God's existence. It was out of His unconditional love for mankind that all was created.

Some people do not believe that God is the Creator

of our world. They accept the so-called big bang theory as an explanation for the creation of the universe. One theory is that the universe started as a single physical entity around 14 billion years ago. Where did that entity come from? There is no definitive answer to that question. The theory is that the immeasurable entity formed and continued to grow in size for billions of years. Eventually, it exploded, discharging an uncountable number of particles which in time resulted in the formation of our universe. Where did the initial entity come from and how was it formed? There is no possible answer to that question. The entity assumption is theory only without any scientific proof. Nor it is universally accepted by the scientific community. My answer to that concept is, prove it. It never has been proven and never can be.

Next, I say prove that God did not create the universe. No, that cannot take place either. So what does all this mean? It means that our acceptance is based on faith, trust, and belief in the Word of God as found in the Holy Bible. His Word gives us the purpose of this life and the promise of everlasting life.

Creation

"In the beginning God created the heavens and the earth. The earth was without form, and void; and darkness was on the face of the deep. And the Spirit of God was hovering over the face of the waters."

—*Genesis 1:1–2*

The Answers

The answers to the question about the existence and omnipotence of God will be found in the Holy Bible, God's masterplan for the salvation of mankind. The entire story of what was, what is, and what will be is all there for everyone who wishes to discover the truth. You owe it to yourself to do so.

I would like to point out that there is unquestionable proof of the validity of both the Old Testament and the New Testament. The Old Testament consists of forty-six books, validated by the Dead Sea Scrolls, which are more than two thousand years old. Many were found intact in caves of Israel along the shores of the Dead Sea. The experts were able to reconstruct around 950 different manuscripts that without a doubt verify the legitimacy of the Old Testament, and more than 5,700 Greek manuscripts verifying the text of the New Testament.

Truth should not be accepted based on likelihood, opportunity, or unfounded belief, for truth and belief

5

are not necessarily the same. You can believe in something, but is what you believe the absolute truth? Its acceptance should not be taken lightly. You owe it to yourself to thoroughly research available information and then form a decision founded on accepted, proven facts. The existence of God is without question well-established and proven in the first book of the Bible alone through creation.

The answers to most of our questions about life on earth and beyond can, as previously stated, be found in the Holy Bible. It is the roadmap on how to get from our earthly existence to our eternal home.

If you were planning a trip and did not have a GPS, you would most likely use a road map. If you wandered off the route, you could get back on course with an accurate map. Our road map to heaven is the Holy Bible. There is no guesswork. It is all there. It shows us how to reach our destination and, most important of all, points out how to get back on course when bad choices are made.

Unfortunately, there are those who dispute the Holy Bible and question its accuracy. Is that because of its religious nature? Is it that today there is a need to question everything religious? I believe so. Yet when the same people read a nonreligious book, acceptance of the written content is usually not questioned. For example, they read a historical book about Ramses the Great, an Egyptian pharaoh, who lived thousands of years before the birth of Christ. His existence and detailed rule are not questioned. Why is that? The obvious reason is because of the available authentic documentation of the facts. Yet we have the written words of people who witnessed Jesus's preaching, miracles, crucifixion, death, and resurrection. Still no acceptance.

The New Testament consists of twenty-seven books and letters. By detailed examination of the Greek manuscripts, it has been proven that 99 percent of the original text can be reconstructed beyond a reasonable doubt.

The Gospel Writers

Jesus with some of the future Gospel writers

Let's look at these authors re the authenticity of their written facts.

Matthew was a tax collector. He was called by Jesus to be an apostle while sitting in his tax collector office located at Capernaum. As Jesus was passing by, He said "Come follow me," which Matthew immediately did without question. Matthew was with Jesus from the beginning of His ministry until Jesus's death. His gospel was written in Hebrew some time before 50 AD. He wrote it for all people, including those who believed in Jesus and those who did not. He wrote it to strengthen believers' spiritual lives and to convince nonbelievers that Jesus was the Messiah. Matthew was martyred in Ethiopia.

Mark was highly active in promoting Christianity. He was a missionary and an assistant to the apostle Peter. His wrote his gospel in around 60 AD to help the Romans understand the teachings of Jesus. Mark's gospel describes the life and many miracles of Jesus as witnessed by him. Mark suffered martyrdom in Egypt, where he was dragged by horses through the streets until he was dead.

Luke was born in Antioch, Syria. He was a physician and among the earliest converts to Christianity. He was a missionary who established numerous Christian communities. He wrote his gospel before 60 AD and based it on facts gathered from those who had witnessed the ministry of Jesus. He was hanged while in Greece because of his faith.

John was a fisherman who lived in Bethsaida. While

Jesus was passing by, he saw John and said to him "Come follow me," which John immediately did. Jesus was remarkably close to John. Before His death, He entrusted him with the care of His mother, the Blessed Virgin Mary. John survived attempted martyrdom in Rome and then was sentenced to work in the mines on the island of Patmos. Eventually, he was freed and became the first bishop of Edessa, Turkey. He wrote his gospel in his old age.

These amazing men were eyewitnesses to Jesus's teachings and/or the numerous miracles He performed. It is all documented in their gospels.

> *"Believe Me that I am in the Father and the Father in Me, or else, believe Me for the sake of the works themselves."*
> *—John 14:11*

Could it be that believing in the Scriptures places too many restrictions on some people's way of life? Or is it that being a spiritual person and belonging to no organized religion is good enough? That would permit an individual to determine what is or is not acceptable and further allow one's opinions to change in order to suit one's needs or desires.

Who Is God?

That question is certainly explainable, but its full understanding is beyond human capability and will remain so until the day we leave this earth.

As the Prophets Foretold

The story of Christianity starts with the many prophecies of the Old Testament and their fulfillment in the New Testament.

Prophecy: Isaiah 7:14

God said He would bring forth a Son from a virgin.

Fulfillment: Matthew 1:18–25

Prophecy: Isaiah 9:6

God said that the Messiah would be the everlasting

Father in human form.

Fulfillment: Acts 1:8

Prophecy: Micah 5:2

God said His Son would be born in Bethlehem

Fulfillment: Matthew 2:1

Prophecy: Psalm 41:9

God said that His Son would be betrayed by a friend who ate with Him.

Fulfillment: Matthew 10:4; John 13:21–22, 25–26

Prophecy: Zechariah 11:12

God said that the price of the betrayer would be thirty pieces of silver.

Fulfillment: Matthew 26:15

Prophecy: Psalm 22:14—20

God said His Son would be crucified.

Fulfillment: Luke 23:33–34

Prophecy: Psalm 16:10

God said that Jesus would rise from the dead.

Fulfillment: Acts 2:31

The above are just a few of the thousands of prophecies that can be found in the Holy Bible. It is important to note that they were made between five hundred to one thousand years before the birth of Christ.

Eyewitnesses

Christianity is an organized religion based on the divine teachings of Jesus Christ, and it has been so for thousands of years. A Christian is not just a word or title to be uttered lightly; it is a way of life. Christ's life on earth has been documented by those who witnessed and recorded the unparalleled greatness of His ministry; however, there were and will continue to be the nonbelievers who question the authenticity of His ministry by claiming He was just a man and not the Messiah.

I would suggest that those who believe that way owe it to themselves to find out the truth by researching the life of Jesus, the best source being the Bible. Could an ordinary man give sight to the blind, heal the cripple, raise people from the dead, and perform numerous other miracles? Obviously, the answer is NO.

Jesus heals ten men with leprosy

"If I do not do the works of My Father, do not believe Me; but if I do, though you do not believe Me,

14

believe the works, that you may know and believe
that the Father is in Me, and I in Him."
—John 10:37–38

Godlessness

Unfortunately, we live in a secular society, a society that occasionally excludes God in the decision-making process. Secularism, as defined by Webster's dictionary, is "a view of life or of any particular matter based on the premise that religion and religious considerations should be ignored or purposely excluded."[1] Another definition is "separation of religious institutions from state institutions and a public sphere where religion may participate, but not dominate," or in other words, limit God's presence in our lives.

"The wicked in his proud countenance does not
seek God; God is in none of his thoughts."
—Psalm 10:4

Just look around and it becomes apparent that religious participation in education and government is becoming, according to many, irrelevant and unnecessary. If that trend continues, it will not be long before the Almighty and His teachings will have little or no place in our society. Let us hope and pray that does not happen, for if it does, it could result in the moral destruction of our country and world society in general. Regardless of what the future brings, God will always exist, and His unconditional love and forgiveness will forever be present.

Being "Spiritual"

Many today, especially the younger generation, have decided not to be members of any organized religion. When the subject is brought up, the response is usually, "I'm a spiritual person." I am not sure if I grasp the entire meaning of that response. What does being a spiritual person mean? Does it mean not acknowledging the commitment to or need of any religion?

Wikipedia defines spirituality as "spiritual, but not religious, is used to self-identify a life stance of spirituality that takes issue with organized religion as the sole or most valuable means of furthering spiritual growth."[2] To me, that means that seeking righteousness through the teachings of any faith is not required to be a spiritual person. The "spiritual person" who does not believe in organized religion does not have a God-given base to build on.

An article by the University of Minnesota states: "Spirituality is a broad concept with room for many perspectives. In general, it includes a sense of connection to something bigger than us and it typically involves a search for the meaning of life. Such as, it is a universal human experience—something that touches us all."[3] That might work if your emphasis is only on an earthly existence with not much concern, if any, about life after death. In comparison, Christians have found the meaning of life in God's Word.

"Individual spirituality" is lacking the direction and

guidance given by God to mankind in a methodized and exact manner. Some of the people I have talked with do not accept the need for structured religion, yet they believe there is a higher being independent of interaction with mankind. If that is so, I would think the next step should be to ask who that being is, why he or she exists, if there is an afterlife—and if so, where, and how this higher being can influence one's life.

Not knowing the true and complete story of what being a Christian means is like receiving a new book, reading a few pages, and then going directly to the last chapter. We will know how it ends but will lack the knowledge of what led up to the ending and possibly forfeit our salvation.

The garden of Eden is a picture of what our life in eternity will be like.

The garden of Eden before sin entered

---

[1] Webster's Third New International Dictionary, Unabridged, s.v. "secularism," accessed July 30, 2020, https://unabridged.merriam-webster.com.

[2] Wikipedia contributors, "Spiritual but not religious," *Wikipedia, The Free Encyclopedia,* https://en.wikipedia.org/w/index.php?title=Spiritual_but_not_religious&oldid=965599943 (accessed July 30, 2020).

[3] University of Minnesota, "What Is Spirituality?" *Taking Charge of Your Health and Wellbeing,* https://www.takingcharge.csh.umn.edu/what-spirituality (accessed July 30, 2020).

2

Choosing Jesus

We were not created to live in the darkness of evil. It is the light of righteousness that will awaken our inner being and guide us through the storms of life.

The Beatitudes show us a way of life that promises salvation for all.

Blessed are the poor in spirit,

For theirs is the kingdom of heaven.

Blessed are those who mourn,

For they shall be comforted.

Blessed are the meek,

For they shall inherit the earth.

Blessed are those who hunger and thirst for righteousness,

For they shall be filled.

Blessed are the merciful,

For they shall obtain mercy.

Blessed are the pure in heart,

For they shall see God.

Blessed are the peacemakers,

For they shall be called sons of God.

Blessed are those who are persecuted for righteousness' sake,

For theirs is the kingdom of heaven.

—Matthew 5:1–12

While on earth, Jesus had both a divine and human nature. He was the earthly extension of God the Father. His divinity always was and forever will be. "There are also heavenly bodies and there are earthly bodies; but the splendor of the heavenly bodies is one

kind, and the splendor of the earthly bodies is another" (1 Corinthians 15:40 NIV). His human nature
was limited to only thirty-three years. During those
years, He experienced human emotions such as happiness, sadness, anger, loneliness, and others, as we
all do. It was during the last part of His ministry that
He told His apostles that He must die and after three
days be bodily raised from the dead.

Jesus ascends into heaven

Forty days later, He would be assumed into heaven.
By doing so, He gave us hope and assurance, through
faith, that on the last day our soul and a new heavenly

body would be united with Him to live in paradise forever.

We Christians believe that Jesus is without question the only begotten Son of God. There are those who do not deny His existence but do deny His divinity. They want to humanize Him by that denial. They accept the morality of His teachings but will not acknowledge the gift of salvation promised to all who believe.

Jesus taught us that salvation is a need of everyone. He taught that God loves all people, forgiveness is for all, and that the way to salvation is through faith. He came to us out of love for all to teach what must be done to achieve our crown of glory. He truly is the Son of God, having said while on earth such things as, "The Father and I are one" (John 10:30). "I say unto you, before Abraham was, I AM" (John 8:58).

Jesus Brings Truth and Light

Jesus lived among us for approximately thirty-three

years, the final three being devoted to His ministry. The events during those three years are detailed in the four Gospels and the other letters of the New Testament. It is through them that the darkness of evil is replaced by the light of truth, which will guide us to everlasting life.

It is because of His death and resurrection that eternal salvation is awaiting mankind. His teachings are not for a few but for all people. There should not be any question regarding their meanings and purpose. Just open your Bible. God's master plan for the salvation of all, and the answers to all aspects of life from the beginning to the final days and beyond, will become clear.

In Mark Cahill's book *One Heartbeat Away,* he asks the question, "If you were to die right now, will you be in heaven?" The most common answers might be that you do not know or that you would be. What is your answer? If it is not yes, then it is time to find out why. Let us look at each one.

I don't know – That answer should be of major concern, and serious consideration should be given to why one does not know. The following two gospel readings should help answer that question: "If you keep My commandments, you will abide in My love" (John 15:10). "The time is fulfilled, and the kingdom of God is at hand. Repent and believe in the gospel" (Mark 1:15).

Jesus was effectually and decisively informing us of the requirements for salvation; namely, seeking forgiveness of sin, believing in His teachings, and obeying His commandments.

Got Time?

Some might think that time is not of the essence, that it is on their side. They are relatively young and believe they do not have to be concerned about the next life quite yet. Religion can wait. What a mistake that can be. We always should be prepared to face our Maker whenever that blessing takes place.

Being prepared is not only about saving oneself. Being prepared means living a life of integrity. When that takes place, the overall effect will most certainly impact not only your life but also the life of others.

Plant the right things in your life today.

"Strive to enter through the narrow gate, for many, I say to you, will seek to enter and will not be able" (Luke 13:24). Jesus makes it clear that not everyone will enter the kingdom of heaven. The reason is sin. When that last breath is taken and it is time to meet our Maker, serious sin will be the determining factor as to where we will spend eternity. Sin is the barrier to the kingdom of heaven. It does not have to be that way because Jesus, through His crucifixion, gave us forgiveness and the promise of salvation, as long as we believe in Him, ask for His forgiveness, and sincerely try to amend our ways. Then and only then will the barrier be removed and the door to heaven will be opened.

God knows we are not perfect, and He does not expect we will be so. What He does expect is that we will try to live our lives according to His teachings. In the end, it will be His judgment that will determine our final destination.

Yes, I would be means you are free of sin. We are all sinners. If you are sorry and have confessed your sin from the heart and asked for His forgiveness, you will be forgiven. Heaven would certainly be empty if it were not for God's forgiveness. Some might say they are not sinners. Is that correct? I do not believe so. Jesus said, "Let he who is without sin cast the first stone" (John 8:7). To make that statement, it is important to understand what is and is not sinful.

Open your Bible to the New Testament, read the Gospels, and the answer will become apparent. For example, "Blessed are the merciful for they will be shown mercy" (Matthew 5:1–12). That blessing refers to those who are kind to others and have a forgiving and compassionate spirit. Is that you? Are you a kind, respectful, forgiving person? Is there someone in your life who you have not yet forgiven? Jesus clearly stated many times if we do not forgive, we will not be forgiven. He also said the way we forgive is the way we will be forgiven. And that's just one sin.

Life on earth is temporary, but life after we leave this earth is eternal. There is no end. We face either eternal salvation or eternal destruction, and the way we live on earth will determine the outcome. I have been asked numerous times what happens when we pass from earthly existence to eternal life. It is a difficult and complex discussion to have, but fortunately, the answers have been given to us by a divine source, Jesus Christ.

Jesus told the repentant criminal who was on a cross beside Him, "Assuredly, I say to you, today you will be with Me in Paradise" (Luke 23:43). At the instant we take our final breath, our eternal destination will become a reality. "The Lord Himself will descend from heaven with a shout, with the voice of an archangel, and with the trumpet of God" (Thessalonians 5:16).

For some, the choice might be to sideline the seriousness of eternity and maybe in the future, examine the promises made by Jesus once again. If that approach is taken, it could be a serious mistake, for we have no control over the finality of our existence on earth.

Many people have the attitude that there is plenty of time to get it right with God. There is a major fallacy in that kind of thinking. We do not know now, nor will we ever know, when our last breath will be taken. That does not mean that end-of-life thoughts should dominate our everyday actions. That is not what God wants us to do. He wants us to enjoy the gift of life but in doing so, realize that it is temporary and that what comes next is forever. "You do not know what will happen tomorrow. For what is your life? It is even a vapor that appears for a little time and then vanishes away" (James 4:14).

What has been accumulated on earth stays on earth. When we leave, it is the way we entered, and that is without anything. "The things which are visible are temporal [just brief and fleeting], but the things which are invisible are everlasting and imperishable" (2 Corinthians 4:18 AMP).

All the material possessions remain and are meaningless as to how we spend eternity. Unfortunately, those whose life is dedicated to the accumulation of material values above all else never give much thought to where eternity will be spent. There will be two choices, eternal salvation or eternal destruction.

Eternal salvation

No Second Chances

"It is appointed for men to die once, but after this,
the judgment."
—Hebrews 9:27

After death, there are no second chances. The only
way to get it right with the Almighty is before we
take our last breath.

At the second coming of Christ, as revealed to us in
the book of Revelation, we will be united with a new
heavenly body. It is not only challenging to think

about but is impossible for us to fully understand. However, because of our faith and trust in Jesus, we willingly accept His Word as truth. It is what He promised us.

Is it worth looking forward to? Would you rather put aside His promise and not have Him be a serious part of your life? That is an individual decision to make, a decision that requires considerable thought and self-examination.

Choose Wisely

After a lot of personal reflection after a business failure, a business owner I know realized that God was giving him another chance to change his thinking of what is important in life. It took time, but eventually he decided that righteousness was going to take priority. It was time to move on, put the past behind, and move forward to achieve the great things God has planned for him.

The Bible tells us to seek righteousness first. By doing so, we will receive our heavenly reward, and the teachings of Jesus clearly show us how that can be accomplished.

- *Salvation is a need of everyone.*
- *God loves all of us unconditionally.*
- *Forgiveness is for all people.*
- *Faith is the way to salvation.*

God gave us the greatest gift imaginable—His Son, Jesus Christ—to help us through the trials of life and to show us the way to the road of righteousness. What a magnificent gift. Jesus taught us that salvation is available to everyone; that God loves all of us regardless of our life status; that forgiveness is for all people; that faith is the way to salvation. Not only will following His teachings save our souls; it will greatly contribute to our having a more harmonious and tranquil earthly existence.

The choice is ours. We can walk in the light with Jesus or walk alone in the darkness.

We will all reap what we sow.

Be Prepared

It is most important that we be prepared, for we do not have any idea when our time will arrive. "You do not know what will happen tomorrow. For what is your life? It is even a vapor that appears for a little time and then vanishes away" (James 4:14).

"We fix our eyes not on what is seen, but on what is unseen, since what is seen is temporary, but what is unseen is eternal."
—1 Corinthians 4:18 NIV

3

Chasing Happiness

"We brought nothing into this world, and it is certain we can carry nothing out."
—*1 Timothy 6:7*

One aspect of life that too much emphasis can be placed on is material accomplishments. In Luke 12:15, Jesus states that life is not measured by what you own. What has been accumulated on earth stays on earth. We leave it the way we entered—without anything.

All the Things

All the material possessions accumulated over our lifetime will remain on earth and are meaningless as to how we spend eternity. They are temporary. Unfortunately for some, not much thought is given to immortality.

There is nothing wrong with having money and the luxuries that go along with it. God created everyone with the ability to lead a productive, worthwhile life. It is our responsibility to accept that gift and, with the help of the Holy Spirit, fulfill it to the best of our ability.

What is wrong is when money becomes so important that spiritual values are compromised and, in some situations, nonexistent. The apostle Paul said money in itself is not evil, it is the love of money that is evil. "The love of money is a root of all kinds of evil, for which some have strayed from the faith in their greediness, and pierced themselves through with many sorrows" (1 Timothy 6:10). In other words, when money becomes a top priority, material and spiritual values become unbalanced. You most likely have heard the expression the more you have, the more you want. How true that is.

A man who only values material treasures

First, seek righteousness, and a proper balance between material and spiritual values will exist. When there are unbalanced values, the door is usually opened for greed to enter. Of course, that does not hold for everyone, but it certainly is the case for many. "Whoever loves money never has enough;

whoever loves wealth is never satisfied with their income. This too is meaningless" (Ecclesiastes 5:10).

The direction of God's plan will never be focused on financial achievement. He will place salvation first. Placing financial success above all else will in most cases result in spiritual disaster. There is nothing immoral with seeking financial gain. What is immoral is the priority assigned to it. If that God-given ability has been given to you, use it, but use it in conjunction with establishing righteousness as the top priority.

"The love of money is the root of all kinds of evil, for which some have strayed from the faith in their greediness, and pierced themselves through with many sorrows" (1 Timothy 6:10). At times, the greed factor enters the picture, and seeking righteousness first is not the chosen approach. It might not start out that way, but when it does take place, values can quickly change. One might say that just because achieving financial success is a top priority, it does not mean it is being greedy. I am sure that is correct for some but not for everyone. The question to consider is when is enough, enough? That is quite personal and can only be answered by self-reflection. Establish your priorities with righteousness being first. If that approach is taken, all else will fall into place both spiritually and emotionally. A clear picture will then evolve with Jesus at the helm.

It is easy for the ratio of both values to get out of sync, especially when the priority is on financial success. Being too busy making money and leading the "good" life can quickly cause a person to lose touch with what is important. Jesus spoke about this issue when a rich man asked Him how to have eternal life. Jesus knew that the man's first love was money and so told him to sell all he had and follow Jesus. The rich man was leading a life that most people can only dream of, but he wasn't ready for what takes place when it is time to leave this earth and come face to face with our Maker. "One's life does not consist in the abundance of the things he possesses" (Luke

12:15).

The rich man loved his money too much.

Steps to Happiness

We all seek happiness, but that is not always the way it turns out. Sometimes, it is because we turn to the material accomplishments that we believe will bring happiness, only to find out how disillusioned we were. First, seek righteousness and a balanced peace of mind will be the reward.

Everyone Knows

- You cannot be all things to all people.

42

- You cannot do all things at once.
- You cannot do all things equally well.
- You cannot do all things better than everyone else.
- Your humanity is showing just like everyone else's.

SO

- You must find out who you are and be that.
- You must decide what comes first and do it.
- You must discover your strengths and use them.
- You must learn not to compete with others, because no one else is in the contest of being you.

THEN

- You will have learned to accept your own uniqueness.
- You will have learned to set priorities and make decisions.

- You will have learned to live with your limitations.

- You will have learned to give yourself the respect that is due.

All will not be perfect. There will be good days and days that are not so good. That is part of life. Once we accept that fact, we can move forward and enjoy the many gifts given to us by God.

Man filled with joy after meeting Jesus

We will then understand that perfect happiness can never exist on earth, for perfect happiness can only be realized in heaven. Can you imagine how magnificent that will be?

But that is the future. How about now? The first step to happiness on earth is to seek righteousness, and that is accomplished by following the teachings of Jesus. Because of our human nature, it will not always be easy, but the reward is certainly worth it.

> I have fought the good fight, I have finished the race, I have kept the faith. Finally, there is laid up for me the crown of righteousness, which the Lord, the righteous Judge, will give to me on that Day, and not to me only but also to all who have loved His appearing.
>
> —Timothy 4:7–8

The apostle Paul wrote the words above in his letter to Timothy—written while he was incarcerated in Rome and awaiting execution because of his faith. Our crown of righteousness, as apostle Paul's, is what Jesus promised, and that is an eternity in paradise.

Jesus gave us the truth to live by. His teachings are

clearly stated throughout the New Testament. In the Gospels, He mentioned the kingdom of heaven more than fifty times. If we believe and embrace His Word, that is where we will receive our crown of glory.

Forgiveness

Jesus taught us to be kind to one another, help those in need, love our fellow man, and above all, to forgive.

There may be circumstances when forgiveness is challenging and problematic, but when it does take place, the result is a spiritual and physical transformation. Physically, it will eliminate the anger and bitterness which, if not managed, can cause serious medical problems. Spiritually, we will experience a peaceful, calming feeling, as well as feel close to God in knowing that this is what He said we must do.

There are many situations when forgiveness can be difficult and at times seem almost impossible. I heard a story about a business owner and his partner that reflects this. Let's call the owner John. John felt an unshakable bond of trust and respect for his second-in-command—a trust and respect one would not expect to find outside family circles. Based on the facts as I know them, that trust and respect quickly evaporated when mismanagement and other related circumstances resulted in financial disaster and, finally, the demise of the company. It was heart wrenching for John to see all that he'd worked so hard for evaporating before his eyes without the possibility of recovery. What was once a bond of trust and respect was now one of bewilderment, anger, and even hatred. It was only when John realized that he needed Jesus to get him through those difficult days, and recovery could only come through Him, that he was able to move forward with his life.

John explained that his life was forever changed during a spontaneous visit to a nearby church. No one was there. He sat down and just let the peace of silence engulf him.

Sitting in the peace of His presence

Words did not have to be spoken, for he knew God was present. The relentless feeling of anger and hatred left him, and in its place was inner peace, calmness, and an understanding of what Jesus wanted him to do—to above all forgive, and that he did. Now it was time to move forward—not alone but with Jesus forever in his life.

"If you forgive men their trespasses, your heavenly Father will also forgive you. But if you do not

forgive men their trespasses, neither will your Father forgive your trespasses."
— *Matthew 7:14–15*

Perfect Happiness

Life is full of complications with underlying difficulties. Without spiritual guidance, our time on earth will be one of continuous turmoil. It will be a life of frustration, confusion, self-indulgence, and little inner peace. Although we seek and find happiness, it will be temporary, for the state of perfect happiness can only be found in heaven. If we have faith and trust and believe, we will be able to cope with the sorrows and disappointments that are natural to our human nature.

God has a lot to say about happiness in His Word.

"Happy are the people whose God is the Lord!"
—*Psalm 144:15*

"Happy is the man who finds wisdom, and the

man who gains understanding."
—Proverbs 3:13

"He who has mercy on the poor, happy is he."
—Proverbs 14:21

"Happy is the man who is always reverent, but he who hardens his heart will fall into calamity."
—Proverbs 28:14

"He who heeds the word wisely will find good, and whoever trusts in the Lord, happy is he."
—Proverbs 16:20

4

Free Will

"The wise man's eyes are in his head, but the fool
walks in darkness."
—Ecclesiastes 2:14 AMP

God gave us an incredibly special gift in free will.
That gift places us above all of creation. It gives us
the ability to reason and make our own decisions.
Having free will does not mean that God will not
take an active role in our lives. He most certainly will
if we believe in Him and ask for His guidance. "The
wicked in his proud countenance does not seek God;
God is in none of his thoughts" (Psalm 10:4).

God will not make our final choices for us. Sometimes the decisions made are regretful. What He will do though, through the power of His Holy Spirit, is influence our decision-making process; but in the end, it will be our choice.

We Always Have the Choice

God, being the Creator of all things, knows from the moment of our birth what our behavior, successes, failures, habits, and everything else will be throughout our entire lives. He knows everything.

I have been told numerous times that if He knows all things, then He knew that Adam and Eve would disobey Him and eat from the tree of knowledge. It does not make any difference whether it was the fruit on a tree or anything else. It was their disobedience to His command that reaped the painful consequences. The reason He did not stop them is because of the gift of free will.

Adam and Eve shut out of the garden of Eden

We, as our first parents, have been created with this gift of free will that puts us on the highest plain of creation. Free will is free choice. Adam and Eve knew that their choice meant going against God's command. They did it anyway and, as we know, the tragic result was their downfall and expulsion from paradise. A little self-reflection will show how every one of us at some time has regretfully used that gift of free will.

Another biblical example of how that marvelous gift was misused is between two of Adam and Eve's sons,

Cain and Abel. Cain was the first human born and was a farmer. His brother Abel was a shepherd and the first human to die. One day, both brothers made their offerings to God, but God favored Abel's offering over Cain's. Cain was so angry that he murdered his brother. He used his gift of free will to commit the sinful choice of murder and because of that choice, God condemned him to a life of wandering. Why didn't Cain just express his feelings of disappointment rather than kill his brother? He knew that there were other choices, but because of his overwhelming anger, he used his free will in an unacceptable and destructive manner.

Before making a choice, one that might have serious consequences, ask yourself, "Is this what God wants me to do? How is it going to affect others as well as myself?" Pray to God for His guidance and in time, you will know the correct direction to take.

Cain kills Abel

Physical and Spiritual Consequences

During my many years as a prison minister, free choice has been a frequent topic of conversation. More than 90 percent of the inmates I have talked with agree that making a bad choice resulted in their incarceration. The real tragedy is that for the most part, spiritual consequences never entered their decision-making process.

One inmate who comes to mind is a man in his late forties. He had been coming to Bible study every

Thursday for about a year because he had finally realized it was time to seek God's help or face the trials of life alone. He wanted to know Jesus, understand His teachings, and, hopefully, change his troublesome ways. He heard about the Bible study program and decided to give it a try.

He was previously incarcerated for ten years and now was in for another year. When he first attended our Bible study, he wanted to move the temptations out of his life that had resulted in his making many bad choices, and he was beginning to realize he could not do it without God's help. As time passed, it became evident that divine intervention was taking place.

In addition to attending the Bible classes, he, his cellmate, and others would discuss Scripture readings and list topics and questions for later class discussion. He was changing spiritually, and his leadership qualities were having a dramatic effect on others. No longer was he gloating about his past endeavors. He now accepted responsibility for his actions and had ample faith and trust in Jesus to believe that change was possible. Not only was it possible, but he could feel its influence in his daily life. His thoughts and actions were no longer being controlled by objectionable choices.

The evil temptations will at times still torment him, but no longer will they dominate his life. At times he might fall, but he will not completely surrender to the grasp of evil. Some battles will be lost. but the war against wrongdoing will eventually be won because he now knows and believes that divine power and strength through the Holy Spirit will enable him to move forward with his newfound life—a life full of hope, faith, trust, and a new beginning.

"No temptation has overtaken you except such as is common to man; but God is faithful, who will not allow you to be tempted beyond what you are able,

but with the temptation will also make the way of
escape, that you may be able to bear it."
—*1 Corinthians 10:13*

Man saying no to temptation

God does have a plan for every human being, but He will not interfere in our lives unless we seek His help. That is all part of the magnificent gift of free will. "Ask, and it will be given to you; seek, and you will find; knock, and it will be opened to you. For everyone who asks receives, and he who seeks finds, and to him who knocks it will be opened" (Matthew 7:7–8).

Privilege

Lately, the word "privileged" has been more and more attached to countless people in our society. It usually is directed toward those who have more than the essentials of life. One definition of privilege is having a special right, advantage, or entitlement. I guess one can say if you live in an affluent community, have advanced education, and are financially comfortable, you can be considered a privileged person. However, I believe that everyone in their uniqueness can be considered privileged, regardless of their station in life, for we are all created in the image and likeness of God. "Then God said, 'Let us make man in Our image, according to Our likeness'" (Genesis 1:26).

All people, by believing in Jesus and accepting His teachings, have a special right: eternity in paradise. What an entitlement that is. All the money in the world cannot buy it. The amazing thing is that entitlement is available to all.

Choose the Life You Live

Being privileged does not mean there is no need to follow the rules and laws that govern all people. We came into this world spiritually equal, and on judgment day we will be judged on the kind of life we led, not on our possessions or prominence.

Wealth does not put anyone above the laws of God or the legal laws of man. That clearly is explained in Luke 16, the story of the rich man and the beggar. The rich man had all he could possibly want, and the poor beggar had little of life's necessities. The rich man would not even give him the leftover scraps of food from the table. Lazarus, the beggar, died and received his crown of glory—an eternity in heaven. The rich man, because of his lack of love and compassion for others, was doomed to spend eternity in hell. He certainly had led a privileged life compared to that of Lazarus, but his love of entitlements resulted in a life of selfishness, greed, and gluttony. "He who oppresses the poor reproaches his Maker, but he who honors Him has mercy on the needy" (Proverbs 14:31).

The selfish man spent eternity in hell.

Today, people tend to make their own rules based on a lack of knowledge with regards to Jesus's teachings. How can a person consider him or herself a Christian without knowing the requirements of Christianity? It is like taking a man who never heard of football and telling him he will be the quarterback for an NFL team. That is absurd! He does not even know the rules of the game. Well, it is the same for one who claims to be a Christian but does not fully know what that entails.

If you are looking for answers, open your Bible. That is where they are.

Many of us go through life believing that our values are above reproach. In fact, we most likely would be offended if anyone thought otherwise. It is about time we accepted the reality that all humans are sinners and have been since the fall of Adam and Eve. It is our belief in Jesus and through His sacrifice on the cross that we have forgiveness of sins and a way to salvation. Unfortunately, many people are not aware of, nor have any interest in knowing more about, either one.

Only God Can Say What Sin Is

I recently was talking to a group of incarcerated men about Christian values with an emphasis on sin and forgiveness. One of the inmates had a look of concern and seemed bewildered. I asked if he was aware that sin can be forgiven. His answer was that he didn't know. As the discussion went on, it sadly became apparent that he was not sure what was or was not a serious sin. Without having any convincing answers, he did not see any reason to change his present way of life. Unfortunately, that is the thinking of many young people, especially those who come from broken homes and are gang associated.

The Bible has the answers we need.

He, as well as others, also had many questions about heaven. The major one being if heaven really exists, and if so, how we get there. The only correct answers relating to heaven come directly from the Word of

God as revealed to us in the Holy Bible. A few of the many excellent Scripture readings that answer this are Revelation 21; Luke 23:43; Psalms 33:13; Philippians 1:21–23.

Joy Forever

Jesus made it quite clear to His apostles that heaven is not fictitious but is a real place with real people who have left this existence with Jesus by their side. Heaven is a place where there is perfect happiness, elimination of all human ailments, and an everlasting reunion with all our loved ones. Most important of all, heaven is the home of Almighty God. No longer will death have a hold on us for death was conquered by Jesus's sacrifice on the cross, His resurrection, and His assumption into heaven.

> *"In My Father's house are many mansions; if it were not so, I would have told you. I go to prepare a place for you. And if I go and prepare a place for you, I will come again and receive you to Myself;*

64

that where I am, there you may be also."

—*John 14:2–3*

In Philippians 3:20, Jesus told us that our citizenship is not of this earth but of heaven. We are here only for a short period of time, whereas heaven will be for eternity. With that being so, how to claim our heavenly citizenship should always be at the forefront, and that is accomplished by choosing to live a life of righteousness. There will be many times during our earthly stay that that might be difficult, but through the grace of our Lord, His forgiveness will free us from the darkness of sin as long as we confess and believe in Him.

That is not saying that everything will be perfect. No, it will not. Although we seek Jesus's advice, our course of action is up to us. That is what the gift of free will is all about. But by placing Jesus first, He will guide us through the decision-making process.

The final decision is ours to make. When we attempt

to do it without His guidance, other factors can become overbearing and result in a regretful outcome. "What profit is it to a man if he gains the whole world, and loses his own soul? Or what will a man give in exchange for his soul?" (Matthew 16:26).

May you focus on Him for your happiness, both now *and* for eternity.

5

Walking with Jesus

*"The wise man's eyes are in his head, but the fool
walks in darkness."*
—*Ecclesiastes 2:14 AMP*

The decision not to walk with Jesus but to walk in
darkness is caused by the misuse of God's gift of wisdom. The result—bad decisions.

Kindness

Walking with Jesus includes showing love, forgiveness, kindness, and humility to all people. Jesus
gives us an example of humility and kindness.

Jesus, knowing that the Father had given all things into His hands, and that He had come from God and was going to God, rose from supper and laid aside His garments, took a towel and girded Himself. After that, He poured water into a basin and began to wash the disciples' feet, and to wipe them with the towel with which He was girded.

—John 13:3–5

We are the same in the eyes of God. It does not matter if we are poor or well-to-do, what our background is, or what the color of our skin is, for everyone's soul is created in God's image and likeness out of His love.

At times, we might think that because of our social status, we are superior to others less fortunate. When that occurs, think of Jesus's act of humility and love He showed by washing the feet of His apostles. In the same way, our everyday actions should demonstrate that we care about our fellow man, regardless of his status, by expressing concern and humility.

The Good Samaritan

Sometimes all it takes is a kind word to change the direction of one's negative attitude. Unfortunately, the opposite is too often the case. In my book *Navigating through the Storms of a Christian Life*, I discuss the power of the human tongue. If not controlled, it can be a deadly weapon.

We know how destructive weapons can be, especially if they are not used for the right reasons. However, there is one weapon far more powerful and destructive than any that man has ever made. It is the human tongue. It is the malicious words spoken, initially by a few, that can spread hatred from a city to a state to a country and finally throughout the world. It is the human tongue that caused the manipulation of mankind many times throughout history, resulting in persecution and attempts, many successful, to annihilate entire ethnic groups.

How about using that powerful weapon in a positive way? Just think what could be accomplished by a few kind words. It would be like a snowball going down a mountain—all the time getting larger and going faster. That is what happens with expressions of kindness, love, and forgiveness. It grows like a pyramid. It will start with one person and spread exponentially. It might start as one simple act of kindness that eventually has a considerable impact on society in general.

Kind acts such as paying for a man's healthcare

Absolute Trust

If I asked what Christianity means to you, your response might be belief in Jesus. Yes, that is a good answer, but even the devil believes in God. "You believe that there is one God. You do well. Even the demons believe—and tremble!" (James 2:19). So do you *absolutely* believe? That means accepting all His teachings without exception. If the answer is yes, then you follow His teachings without questioning their importance or being selective. One example is forgiveness, which I talked about earlier. I cannot

71

count the number of people who, in discussions I have had, were adamant about forgiveness being selective. Once again, if you call yourself a Christian, you must have complete trust in Him and obedience to all His teachings.

The following story is an example of the difference between believing and absolutely believing. In the year 1859, there lived the greatest tightrope walker in the world, a Frenchman named Charles Blondin. He planned to be the first man to cross Niagara Falls walking on a cable. The distance of the crossing was 1,100 feet, and the cable was three inches in diameter. The height above the rocks and water was 160 feet— about nine-tenths as tall as The Leaning Tower of Pisa. Thousands of people from all over the world came to witness this first-ever daredevil feat. Charles Blondin was not using any safety equipment, so if he misstepped, it would certainly result in his death. That did not happen, and he was successful in making the crossing.

The crowds were cheering him as they saw history being made. He then asked if they believed he could cross back to the other side pushing a wheelbarrow. The spectators shouted, "Yes, you are the greatest. We know you can do it." And he did. Once again, there was a joyous eruption of praise from all the spectators.

He then shouted, "Do you think I can cross to the other side with a person in the wheelbarrow?" Once again, the spontaneous response was yes. Charles then shouted back, "Who will volunteer to sit in the wheelbarrow?" He had no takers. They believed in his greatness but did not believe beyond question. If they had sincerely believed, he would have had many volunteers. Is it time to ask yourself if you believe without question?

Moving Mountains

Jesus tells what a small amount of faith can accomplish: "If you have faith as a mustard seed, you will say to this mountain, 'Move from here to there,' and it will move; and nothing will be impossible for you" (Matthew 17:20).

The centurion's faith healed his servant.

We all have mountains to move in our everyday lives. They could include excessive alcohol consumption, drugs, lack of forgiveness, unfaithfulness, greed, gossip, gambling, and on and on. What Jesus is revealing to us is that with just a little bit of faith, we can begin the process of moving those harmful mountains out of our lives.

Can you imagine how our lives would be if we had

more than a little bit of faith? Once again, it will take faith, belief, and trust in Him. He is always there for us. Just ask for His help, be persistent and patient, and above all, believe. "Ask, and it will be given to you; seek, and you will find; knock, and it will be open to you. For everyone who asks receives, and he who seeks finds, and to him who knocks it will be opened" (Matthew 7:7–8).

We are human beings and therefore do not have, and can never achieve, perfection. There will be times when the strength of our faith will be tested. When that takes place, let us never forget that divine help is available for the asking. We are never alone, and our Shepherd is always present to guide us back to righteousness.

What is difficult for us to understand is that our timeframe for things to change for the better is not necessarily the same as God's. "But, beloved, do not forget this one thing, that with the Lord, one day is as a thousand years and, a thousand years as one day"

(Peter 3:8). So do not give up. Keep asking for His help. It might take longer than you hoped, and His answer might not be what you asked for, but trust in the Lord. It will happen if you are persistent and truly believe in Him.

Sometimes what we ask for is not what God has planned for us. We, on the other hand, will never understand why things happen unless we have an abundance of faith and trust in Him.

In my book *Navigating through the Storms of a Christian Life,* I state:

> Life without Jesus is like being on a boat without a rudder in a violent and powerful storm. There is no way to stay on course. The boat goes this way and that way depending on the wind, waves, and currents. No steady direction can be maintained, and disaster is always present. When we bring Jesus into our lives, our course of righteousness becomes clear. He is our rudder, and through His

grace, the storms of life can be confronted and de-feated.

Jesus leads us through the storms of life.

We always need Jesus, not only when things are not going well but *always*. Christianity is not just a word. It is a way of life.

> "Peace I leave with you, My peace I give to you; not as the world gives do I give to you. Let not your heart be troubled, neither let it be afraid."
> —John 14:27

"I am with you always, even to the end of the age."

—John 28:20

6

Obedience

Abraham obeyed My voice and kept My charge,
My commandments, My statutes, and My laws.
—Genesis 26:4–6

To have a better realization of your relationship with God, ask yourself, "Am I trying to lead a life according to the Ten Commandments and the teachings of His only begotten Son, Jesus Christ?" In other words, are we seeking righteousness first or does that only take place when circumstances do not go our way and we then realize His help is needed?

If you first seek righteousness, not only will you have

a superior relationship with God, but you will have a clearer understanding of how to cope with the difficult times common to all mankind.

Abraham—a man of righteousness

If the wicked man turns from all his sins which he has committed, keeps all My statutes, and does what is lawful and right, he shall surely live: he shall not die. None of the transgressions which he has committed shall be remembered against him; because of the righteousness which he has done, he shall live.

— Ezekiel 18:21–22

God's gift, the Ten Commandments, is His master plan for our salvation. As we have seen, He is merciful and forgiving; however, we will face His wrath if His law is willfully disregarded and forgiveness is not sought.

The Great Flood

An example of God's wrath was the great flood, resulting in the destruction and end of all life on earth, the only human exception being Noah and his family.

Through the gift of free will, mankind had disregarded God, put aside righteousness, and idolized evil. God was deeply saddened by the wickedness and evil actions of His creation. That was not what He had intended when He spoke the world into existence. However, He was pleased with the righteousness of Noah.

God instructed Noah to build an ark large enough for his family "and of every living thing of all flesh you shall bring two of every sort into the ark, to keep them alive with you" (Genesis 6:19). When God's instructions were completed, forty days of torrential rain engulfed the earth, resulting in the great flood and the death of all living beings and creatures. That catastrophic event took place approximately 1,656 years after the creation of man, according to the Bible and its well-documented historical events.

The great flood

The End of Times

God has been very patient with man's behavior for many thousands of years since the great flood. It should make one wonder if we are trending toward the same catastrophic devastation resulting in a similar end. I believe the answer is yes and that it could happen sooner rather than later. The end of times will again take place, but only God knows when that will be. Jesus tell us that "of that day and hour no one knows, not even the angels of heaven, but My Father only" (Matthew 24:36). Does it make sense to be prepared for that day? I certainly believe so.

Take the time to read the words of Jesus in Matthew 24:1–44. If only all people would believe those sacred words, maybe change could take place. What we do know for sure is that when it happens, it will not be caused by another great flood because God promised Noah "Never again shall there be a flood to destroy the earth" (Genesis 9:11).

His Covenant

God created us, and everything that ever was is now and ever will be. He established His relationship and

His covenant with mankind through the Ten Commandments. They provide us with a divine doctrine to be honored and obeyed for life.

God's covenant of structure and guidance gives us the means of achieving inner peace and eternal salvation. His only begotten Son, Jesus, taught us the importance and necessity of obeying His commandments. He knew that, because of our humanity, at times we might falter and consequently sin; but if we believe in Him, ask for forgiveness, and follow His teachings, we will be saved. "For the Son of Man has come to seek and to save that which was lost" (Luke 19:10).

God's Commandments

1. I am the Lord your God; you shall have no other false gods before me.
2. You shall not take the name of the Lord your God in vain.
3. You shall keep holy the Sabbath day.
4. You shall honor your father and your mother.

5. You shall not kill.

6. You shall not commit adultery.

7. You shall not steal.

8. You shall not bear false witness against your neighbor.

9. You shall not covet your neighbor's wife.

10. You shall not covet your neighbor's goods.

—Exodus 20:1–26

One might ask how important the Ten Commandments are. Here is what Jesus had to say about that: "If you want to enter into life, keep the commandments" (Matthew 19:17). "Do not think that I came to destroy the Law or the Prophets. I did not come to destroy but to fulfill" (Matthew 5:17).

I believe that answers the question.

Another example of how important they are is what God said to Joshua prior to the Israelites crossing the Jordan River. God instructed Joshua to have His people recite the Ten Commandments frequently less they forget them. The same should hold true for us.

Moses receives the Ten Commandments.

Saying the commandments of God, praying, reading the Bible, and studying the teachings of Jesus will provide a solid foundation to grow our faith, hope, and trust in the Almighty. Faith is the basis of Christianity, and hope is a spiritual pillar of faith.

"Through [Jesus] also we have access by faith into
this grace in which we stand, and rejoice in hope
of the glory of God."
—Romans 5:2

The Journey Home

Since the beginning of this book, I have covered a lot about the necessity of having Jesus in our lives. Now I'd like to talk about those who drift away from Christianity and then, because of what can be considered a series of events—some tragic, eventually find their way home.

To a great extent, the journey back kind of parallels Luke 15:11–32, the parable of the lost son. This gospel reading is about a young man who came from a wealthy family, a man who was not satisfied with just working for his father. He wanted to do his thing, travel, and experience life as he saw fit. The only way that could take place would be if he could have his inheritance immediately and not wait until the death of his father. The amount would be substantial and would allow him to experience the lifestyle of his choosing. The son was young and intended to enjoy an affluent life to its fullest without thinking of possible future consequences.

The son explained his wishes to his father and reluctantly, his father consented. Sure enough, after living a lifestyle of squandering and excessiveness, his inheritance was gone. To make matters worse, a severe famine engulfed the country he was in. His life was now a disaster. No money, no food, and rags for clothes. He was destitute. It was only then that he realized the choices he had made were not good ones. He wanted to go home but did not know if his father would welcome him back. He soon found out how strong his father's forgiveness and love were. His father was waiting for his son's return home with open arms.

Every time we disregard Jesus by going against His will, we become the lost son. We finally realize that without Him, life is an existence of emptiness and frustration. We might have left Jesus, but He will never leave us. He will be waiting for us to return and when we do, we will be welcomed back with open arms, love, and forgiveness.

The prodigal son is welcomed home.

God is not going to decide for us. If we are patient and have faith, His direction will become obvious and indisputable. It will then be up to us to take the next step.

The path our Lord wants us to follow might not be anything close to what we thought would be the way. Rely on Him for He knows what is best. Once again, seek righteousness first and there will be little doubt as to what path to follow.

"Blessed are those who hunger and thirst for

righteousness, for they shall be filled."

—Matthew 5:6

"Seek first the kingdom of God and His righteous-ness, and all these things shall be added to you."

—Matthew 6:33

7

When Bad Things Happen

Great is your love toward me;
you have delivered me from the depths,
from the realm of the dead.
—Psalm 86:13 NIV

Some people will say if there is a God, why doesn't He stop all the bad things that happen. Can He? The answer is yes, He can, and He will—once we as a nation accept Him, believe in Him, and ask for His divine help.

David trusted the Lord.

Why Me?

How many times have you asked yourself the question "Why me, God?" The answer probably is, "I do not know," but people ask it a lot. Most of the time, people ask it when they are going through situations of an unpleasant nature and they want someone to blame or, when appropriate, they don't want to take responsibility for their choices. Unfortunately, we usually blame God. That is the easy way out because He is not going to physically appear and dispute our claim.

No, unpleasant situations are not His fault. He is a loving God, a God who loves you unconditionally. Do you know anyone else who loves you unconditionally? "The righteous cry out, and the Lord hears and delivers them out of their troubles. The Lord is near to those who have a broken heart and saves such as have a contrite spirit" (Psalm 34:17–18).

The most common "why me" relates to the self—illness or death of a loved one. There are many people who, before those circumstances, were strong in their faith, but now they feel that God has let them down. In extreme cases, they even doubt the existence of God. They continually ask the same questions. "Why did He let it happen?" "Why weren't my prayers answered?" "Why didn't a miracle take place?" Then the unfortunate might follow—religion no longer has a high priority or, sadly, any priority at all.

Bad things are not God's fault, and we can see that is true when we understand God's participation in our life first and foremost.

Man questioning God

We Have Hope

At times, horrific events take place, resulting in extreme distress and anxiety. Events such as natural disasters, illness, the death of a family member or friend, losing a job, or marital problems often aren't anyone's fault. It is life. It is part of being a human being. Many events are acts of nature that we have little or no control over, such as earthquakes, hurricanes, and tornados. It would be extremely difficult to confront and cope with any of those dreadful situations without faith and trust in God.

Having endurance and fortitude is essential, for they will play an important part in the acceptance process which, in turn, is necessary for our spiritual and physical well-being. At times, events can be so overwhelming we choose to give up, but before doing so, we need to seek God's help. If not, we will be missing out on what He has to offer. Anything good is worth fighting for. We are not alone. We all are in the hands of God, and He will provide the strength needed to get through whatever the hardships are. Just ask for His help.

> *"Come to me, all you who are weary and burdened, and I will give you rest."*
> *—Matthew 11:28 NIV*

God's Timing

In the Old Testament book of Ecclesiastes, Solomon pointed out that man will experience many emotional events during his life—times of pleasure and times of sorrow. "To everything there is a season, a time for every purpose under heaven" (Ecclesiastes 3:1).

Unfortunately, we live in a society where solutions and positive results must be immediate. Things do not work that way with God. "Beloved, do not forget this one thing, that with the Lord one day is as a thousand years, and a thousand years as one day" (2 Peter 3:8). Trust in Him, have hope, and most importantly, believe. It might seem that there are more down days than up days, but persevere, for if you do so, there soon will be a reversal. Why? Because you will have realized that God is in charge and that He will get you through your difficulties, no matter how overpowering they might seem.

In a way, the ups and downs can be compared to a military conflict in which many battles are fought. Some are won and others are lost. In the end, the victor will not be chosen based on the number of battles won but on who, in spite of the odds, believed in victory, fought on, and did not give up.

Possessing faith and trust in the Lord will certainly help guide us through the numerous struggles and frustrations common to man. Once we acknowledge God's existence and submit to His will, He will give us the strength to handle all things.

He is our Good Shepherd.

Knowing God

Having a meaningful relationship with God will be a lifechanging event. The euphoria experienced through His grace and love will be intense and ever-lasting. He is our Father, our Creator, and the Creator of everything that ever was, exists now, or will exist in the future.

Being our heavenly Father, He is always present, waiting for us to seek His unwavering help. There is nothing that has or will have occurred in our lives that could turn Him away from us. His love for us is all-powerful, unconditional, everlasting, and beyond reproach. We are the ones who at times push Him away. Do not let that happen! Tell Him that you do not understand why the confusing and distressing events have entered your life and that you need Him to guide you and help you through those troubling times. The more you pray, the closer you will become to God and the stronger your faith and trust in Him will be.

"You have made known to me the paths of life;
you will fill me with joy in your presence."
—*Acts 2:28*

The words and music of *The Prayer*, a song by Celine Dion and Andrea Bocelli, is an example of asking for God's help, grace, and guidance through life experiences. It compassionately points out our dependence and trust in Him. The song is a request of God to watch over us, help us, guide us, keep us safe, light the way, lead us, give us faith, and bring us people to love and who will love us in hard times. Listen to it if you can.

Spiritual Fitness

Faith and trust are spiritual objectives that will help our relationship with God to develop into one that is enduring and unyielding.

In a way, the effects of growing in faith and trust are like the effects of physical exercise. With an established fitness goal, the more a person exercises, the stronger they will get and the closer they will be to achieving their goal. Spiritually, we seek righteousness, and that goal is an eternity in paradise. The more we pray, the closer we get to achieving our objective and, in the process, we will experience consistent growth in our faith and trust in God. "Without faith it is impossible to please Him, for he who comes to God must believe that He is, and that He is a rewarder of those who diligently seek Him" (Hebrews 11:6).

Victory

Faith and trust in God can produce unimaginable results. In 1 Samuel, we read about a young man named David who saved Israel from slavery by defeating a giant of a man, Goliath.

David was a young man whose job it was to tend his father's sheep, but he heard about Goliath's challenge to Israel to a fight. This matchup was to be a battle till death. If Goliath won, the Israelites would become slaves of the pagan Philistines. If David was the victor, the Philistines would be slaves of the Israelites.

Goliath

Goliath was a Philistine and a pagan. He was a proven warrior known for his military valor. He was approximately seven feet tall, very muscular, and powerful. David was a nonwarrior of average height and rather on the slight side. David was the only Israelite willing to fight Goliath and thus save his people.

By all standards, David should have easily been defeated, but he was not. He had complete faith and trust in God. He believed that through God's divine intervention, he would be the victor, and he was.

David kills Goliath.

Just think about the changes that could take place in our lives if we placed our faith and trust in the Lord, asked for His help, and believed. Like David, sometime the odds will be against us and overpowering, but we will always have the strength to win our battles as long as we walk the walk with Jesus at our side.

Nothing Is Impossible with God

Life can be exceedingly difficult at times, for some more than others. Trying to get through those problematic and stressful times without help can seem impossible. Some days can be exceedingly troublesome and at times, it might appear that there is no way out. That does not have to be the case. We have Jesus, our Savior, waiting for us to ask for his help.

> Ask, and it will be given to you; seek and you will find; knock, and it will be opened to you. For everyone who asks receives, and he who seeks finds, and to him who knocks it will be opened

> —Matthew 7:7–8

Believe and trust in Him. His unconditional love will drape over you and will become a cloak of spiritual strength and guidance. He will give you a new beginning. What seemed impossible will now be possible. Most likely, it will not take place overnight, but with Jesus in your life, it will happen, and when it does, you will have a completely different perspective on the meaning of life and the direction to be taken.

"The things which are impossible with men are possible with God."

—Luke 18:27

8

God-Given Capabilities

The Spirit of God has made me, and the breath of the
Almighty gives me life.
—Job 33:4

Accept who you are. Be yourself and enjoy the gift of being you. Each of us was created with the ability to achieve the maximum of our God-given capabilities. Whatever that gift is, it should not be wasted. Establish a goal with righteousness first and all else will fall into place. It will be a grand awareness of success, knowing whatever the results, you did your best.

Sometimes the difficulty in following God is just in

getting started. That might be attributed to a lack of believing in oneself. If we believe we cannot achieve, we never will. What I am saying is, a positive attitude is a necessity.

Self-Esteem

Occasionally, because of a past happening, the lack of a positive attitude can be attributed to the loss of self-respect. That can cause one to have negative personal feelings. Also, serious sin can be a major cause of low self-esteem.

Having been a prison minister for many years, I have talked with numerous inmates who have negative attitudes and low self-esteem. In many instances, they want to change but do not know where to start. They realize that what they did was wrong but did it anyway. The temptation was so overpowering that there was no desire to fight it. They just let it be and accepted the consequences. The result usually ended in being arrested. They wanted help but did not know how to go about getting it. Their life was full of un-certainty, and they faced years or even a lifetime in prison.

Many of the inmates did not believe they had the willpower to break away from lawless actions. They needed a role model—one who they could trust and believe in. In time, some finally realized that that person is now and always will be Jesus Christ.

One thirty-year-old man told me he had been in and out of prison since he was thirteen years old. He said that he expected it would be that way for the rest of his life. He kind of believed in Jesus but did not un-derstand what true belief meant. He did not under-stand the importance of faith and trust in the Lord. In his case, it most likely stemmed from the lack of one of the main necessities of childhood—family guidance. When that is lacking, a young person will seek a family bond elsewhere. Depending on circum-stances, that bond usually ends up being found in a gang. The gang then becomes the family, and it is all downhill from there.

In a gang, the laws of society and religion become meaningless. Being part of one results in a life of crime, and the individual usually does not see any way out. For all practical purposes, that person soon becomes a ward of the prison system.

Starting Over

Many incarcerated inmates want to have Jesus in their lives but do not know that much about Him. They lack understanding of what it means to be a believer. Maybe you, reading these words, might feel the same way.

It is through desire, prayer, and Bible study that the process begins. That magnificent book, the Bible, God's master plan for the salvation of mankind, gives you the purpose of life and a promise of an afterlife. It has all the answers you need to begin your journey with Jesus at the helm.

The words of Jesus give life.

A few of the many questions I have been asked are:

How do I have faith and trust in Jesus?

Fear not, for I am with you;

Be not dismayed, for I am your God.

I will strengthen you,

Yes, I will help you,

I will uphold you with My righteous right hand.

—Isaiah 41:10

Faith and trust in Jesus come from knowing and believing in Him. Knowing Him is the acceptance that He always was and always will be. Believing in Him is the acknowledgment and acceptance of His teachings without exception. Once you can say "I know Jesus and I believe in Him," faith and trust will follow.

What are His teachings?

God so loved the world that He gave His only begotten Son, that whoever believes in Him should not perish, but have everlasting life.

—John 3:16

Jesus's teachings are found in the Beatitudes. They provide a way of life that promises us an inner peace during our earthly trials and the eternal reward of salvation. In them, Jesus told us to love and forgive all people; to be kind, humble, and not judge; to treat people with respect and love.

How do I make the right choices?

Trust in the Lord with all your heart,

And lean not on your own understanding;

In all your ways acknowledge Him,

And He shall direct your paths.

—Proverbs 3:5–6

Ask Jesus for guidance. He knows that life sometimes presents itself with difficult choices. Even though they might not be life-altering ones and would not seem significant to others, they are important to whoever is experiencing them. If you want a second opinion, He is always available and waiting to help. He who knows you far better than you know yourself. Believe and trust in Him.

How do I break bad habits?

Do not love the world or the things in the world.

If anyone loves the world, the love of the Father is not in him.

—1 John 2 15

Breaking bad habits can certainly be challenging and probably will require guidance. The longer the obsession has existed, the stronger its influence will be. I believe the best way to break a habit is by forming another one to take its place. Let that new one be unbreakable faith and trust in God. Only then will divine guidance provide the abundant grace essential for the elimination of the unacceptable habit from your life. It will not happen immediately, but through perseverance of prayer and desire for change, it will take place.

How do I move on with life?

A cheerful heart is good medicine,
   but a crushed spirit dries up the bones.

—Proverbs 17:22

The lack of self-confidence can prevent a person from moving forward and achieving a life full of promise within their God-given abilities. Sometimes the lack of self-confidence comes from past failures, which certainly can result in a defeatist attitude. We all have failures in our lives. Some are greater than others, but they should not stop us from moving forward to achieve the success and greatness that is there for us. Be a successful person who will learn from failures and move forward with newfound self-confidence. If not, life will pass you by and leave you with regrets of what could have taken place.

Why should I forgive?

If you forgive other people when they sin against you, your heavenly Father will also forgive you. But if you do not forgive others their sins, your Father will not forgive your sins.

—Matthew 6:14–15 NIV

Forgiveness is a must for a Christian. If we do not forgive, we will not be forgiven. When an individual finds it difficult to forgive, think of Jesus being crucified. Through all His suffering, He asked God the Father to forgive those who were killing Him. When we forgive, a spiritual and physical healing process takes place. Spiritually, we are cleansing our soul and fulfilling one of the most essential requirements for achieving salvation. Physically, we are healing the stressful effects of ongoing anger and possibly revenge.

How do I acquire wisdom?

If any of you lacks wisdom, you should ask God, who gives generously to all without finding fault, and it will be given to you.

—James 1:5

Wisdom is a gift from Almighty God. All we must do is ask for it and through the power of the Holy

Spirit, it will be granted. Wisdom is using our God-given ability to act using knowledge, experience, understanding, and common sense. Be sincere and ask from the heart.

Once there is an understanding of the answers to those questions, life will forever be changed. It will not happen overnight, but be patient, for it will happen.

The Process of Change

I once talked with an inmate who had been incarcerated for over one year and was awaiting trial. His life of crime had finally caught up with him. I never ask what charges a person is facing, and seldom do they volunteer that information. They, for the most part, are regretful of their actions and want to change their troublesome way of life.

One of my goals is to give spiritual guidance that will hopefully help the individual handle the stress and uncertainties of being incarcerated. The physical and mental effects caused by incarceration take a monumental toll on most of the inmates. Having faith, hope, and trust in the Lord will be a major step forward in providing the spiritual strength to get through their present and future uncertainties.

Man in prison

The inmate in question asked if we could talk about what he was facing and how he planned to handle it. He was very calm and told me that he accepted a plea bargain of ninety-nine years without the possibility of parole. That was shocking, but what he further said was even more so. He accepted that sentence because he knew he was guilty and knew that if the case went to trial, the outcome would be the same. Obviously, his crimes were serious felonies. Knowing this, he did not want his family to go through the hardship of his trial.

During the one year since his arrest, he faithfully attended Bible study classes and began the process of dedicating his life to Jesus. His desire to know Jesus and His teachings continually increased. It became obvious to me that his closeness to Jesus was changing his life. He no longer was the same person. He now had faith in the Lord and believed that he could handle being in prison for the rest of his life. This was difficult but encouraging to hear—he was a young man who would never have freedom again. He went on to say that he planned to be a prison minister, to teach Bible classes, and to bring Jesus into the lives of other inmates. If that is so, not only will he be saved but most likely, many others will be saved through his efforts. The Lord, through the power of the Holy Spirit, will give him the spiritual strength he needs to be His disciple.

The inmate also believed that if it was God's will, maybe sometime in the future his sentence would be changed, and he would be considered for parole. Through his faith he has hope, and for Christians, hope is a spiritual pillar of faith.

One's Spiritual Life Can Be Dramatically Changed

Another inmate in my Bible study class had previously served ten years in prison. Now he was back in jail for what I believe to be a violation of parole. When he first attended Bible study, it became apparent that he wanted to change his life but was not sure he could do it. One day we were discussing the loss of salvation due to sin. He asked what sins would be serious enough to keep him out of heaven. That question has been asked of me many times during my years as a prison minister. The answer is clearly stated by Jesus in the following Bible verses: "If you want to enter into life, keep the commandments" (Matthew

19:17). "Most assuredly, I say to you, if anyone keeps my Word he shall never see death" (John 8:51).

In summary, salvation requires keeping the Ten Commandments and obeying the teachings of Jesus. We are all sinners and at times will fall. However, through the grace of our Lord, if we seek His forgiveness, repent, and sincerely try to amend our ways, we will be forgiven.

> *"If we confess our sins, He is faithful and just to forgive us our sins and to cleanse us from all unrighteousness."*
> *—1 John 1:9*

The inmate in question read his Bible daily, and over time, it became obvious that his faith and trust in the Almighty were growing. He was beginning to understand that he was not alone and that with faith and trust in our Lord, he could, in time, defeat the demons that had controlled his life.

God helps us fight our battles.

Through the teachings of Jesus, he was beginning to gain self-confidence in being able to change his dark ways. There was a new life waiting for him and now it was within his reach. Over that year, he read the entire New Testament and a few books of the Old Testament. As time went by, he set up group discussions with other inmates. His life was changing. He became a new person. He knew there would be difficult times ahead, times when he would succumb to sinful temptations, but he also knew that if he was sorry, sincerely tried to conquer those temptations, and asked for forgiveness, he would be forgiven. Through his prayer and understanding of the values of the Christian life, he was gradually building a spiritual shield against the evil side of mankind.

Gain Understanding

*"I have filled him with the Spirit of God, in wisdom, in **understanding**, in knowledge, and in all manner of workmanship."*
—*Exodus 31:3*

Before reading the Bible each day:

1. Ask the Holy Spirit to give you the wisdom to understand His sacred words.
2. Take your time. Read a sentence or a paragraph and then dwell on it.
3. Ask God what He is telling you.
4. Once you have a clear understanding, read on.

As this process continues, your life will slowly change. The meaning of your life will become clearer, and life on earth will be more rewarding, not only to yourself but to others. More importantly, the meaning and glory of your heavenly destiny will become a joyful reality.

A Well-Balanced Life

Both spiritual and material values are fundamental for achieving a well-balanced life. If you have the God-given ability to acquire the finer things, go for them, but go for them with Jesus as your partner. By doing so, righteousness will always become a priority in the decision-making process.

The ability to achieve and be successful is a gift from God. He gave each of us the intelligence and talent to achieve success within our own individual capabilities. It does not matter whether that something is being a janitor or a brain surgeon; you should accept the gift, whatever it is, without longing for what someone else has but with pride in what you have accomplished.

Each person is unique in capabilities but identical in God. We all have a soul created in the image and likeness of God. That puts all of us on an equal basis at the time of our eternal judgment. It will not matter how financially successful you were or what material assets you acquired. When we leave this earth, we will go the way we came into it—without anything. "Life does not consist in an abundance of possessions" (Luke 12:15 NIV).

Now comes eternity. What will then matter is the kind of a person you were and, most important of all, DID YOU BELIEVE? If we follow God's teachings, it will result in a more balanced life on earth and certainly will be a major accomplishment toward achieving one's final goal of eternal salvation.

Success

Most people have the desire to succeed in their endeavors, but some lack the necessary self-confidence to accept the challenge. Does that sound familiar?

Could that be you? There are many reasons for this mindset. One of the contributing factors can be related to the magnitude leading up to and after a catastrophic event. The easy way out is just to quit, but you don't grow that way.

God will help us succeed.

Failure can be a prelude to success only if its reason is completely understood. It is during that process of failing that excuses for the troublesome incident are made. Generally, there is a sequence of events contributing to the failure, but they were disregarded without much thought being given to the possible consequences. Not accepting any fault but blaming everything and everyone else *but* you can lead to depression and an overwhelming perception of low self-esteem. It implies you are helpless when you had the power to choose righteousness every step of the way.

It does not have to be that way, and only you can prevent those debilitating developments from taking place.

1. Learn from the past.
2. Accept your capabilities.
3. Move forward to a rewarding future.

Once that takes place, you then will have learned how to use your God-given uniqueness in special and productive ways.

Hope in God

When difficult times come and all looks bleak, do not give up. Rely on the gift of hope. It is through hope given to us by the Almighty that despair can be conquered. Hope frees us from the chains of desperation, anguish, and gloom. It provides a way to move forward with a positive attitude, propelling us to physical and spiritual victory.

Move forward and do not dwell on the past. We all make mistakes, some more serious than others. That is being human. The only perfect being is God. Accept that no matter how much we strive for perfection, it never will happen, for perfection can only be realized in heaven. It's by walking with a perfect God that we can see a future filled with hope because He's leading us to it.

9

Our Foundation

*Whoever hears these sayings of Mine, and does
them, I will liken him to a wise man who built
his house on the rock.*
—Matthew 7:24

Spiritual help is always available for the asking, which
is prayer. The power of prayer can never be over-
stated. Its effect is one of spiritual strength, wisdom,
and understanding. All three are instrumental in
providing a solid foundation of faith and trust to
build on.

Prayer is a vital and necessary part of Christian life.

Thomas Merton once wrote a powerful prayer of hope and trust in God.

> My Lord God, I have no idea where I am going. I do not see the road ahead of me. I cannot know for certain where it will end. Nor do I really know myself, and the fact that I think that I am following your will does not mean that I am actually doing so. But I believe that the desire to please you does, in fact, please you. And I hope that I have that desire in all that I am doing. I hope that I will never do anything apart from that desire. And I know that if I do this you will lead me by the right road, though I may know nothing about it. Therefore, will trust you always though I may seem to be lost and in the shadow of death. I will not fear, for you are ever with me, and you will never leave me to face my perils alone.
>
> —Thomas Merton, *Thoughts in Solitude*[1]

It is from the grace received through prayer that we

can start the process of developing a solid foundation of Christian values. Once that takes place, we will be fortified with sufficient spiritual strength to help us withstand the storms of evil.

Jesus pointed out the requirement of having a strong Christian foundation in His parable about building a house on the rock (Matthew 7:24–26).

The parable is about two men, one of whom built his house on rock and the other who built his house on sand. Once the strong winds and rain came, the house built on sand was quickly destroyed because it had a weak foundation. Regardless of how severe the storms were, the house built on rock survived because it had a solid foundation. In both examples given to us by Jesus, the storms represent the evil every human being is subjected to. With a strong foundation of faith, trust, and belief, we will not succumb, for evil will have been defeated.

A house built on sand will be washed away.

Whoever hears these sayings of Mine, and does them, I will liken him to a wise man who built his house on the rock: and the rain descended, the floods came, and the wind blew and beat on that house; and it did not fall, for it was founded on the rock.

But everyone who hears these sayings of Mine, and does not do them, will be like a foolish man who built his house on the sand: and the rain descended, the floods came, and the winds blew and beat on that house; and it fell.

And great was its fall.

—Matthew 7:24–27

I would like to conclude this book by quoting from sections of the most descriptive and heartbreaking story of Jesus's crucifixion that I have ever read, published by Keep Believing Ministries.

The Crucifixion of Jesus
Told by a Roman Soldier

I had never seen anything like that day in my time spent with the Roman Legion in Jerusalem. I had helped perform many executions, but this one was different. This day there were three men condemned to die.

The sentence for each was death by crucifixion. We tied the large crossbeams of wood across the backs of each of the condemned. Their arms were outstretched on the wood demonstrating to everyone what was going to happen to them. Everyone

131

knew where we were headed. There was this hill called The Skull where the executions took place.

Several splinters from the wood slivered deep into their skin. The first man hollered curses at the crowd. The second man was the opposite. He cried out for mercy. As the third man came by, I heard the whispers going through the crowd. I overheard that this was Jesus. He did not look like the criminal he was supposed to be. Also, on his head, there was a wreath of thorns. Each one had dug deeply into his flesh covering his head in blood. He was so badly beaten that the pain had to be unbearable. I glanced at Him and saw such a peaceful look in his eyes. This peace did not make sense. Didn't he realize that He was about to die one of the most gruesome deaths possible? Did He know that He would die from lack of air as He tried to pull Himself up, but his nail-pierced wrists lacked the strength? Finally, His lungs would fill with fluid and He would die. The weight of the cross was too much for Him. I grabbed someone from the crowd and told him to carry the cross.

Jesus carrying the cross

Finally, we reached the place of execution. The sound of the nails being hammered echoed throughout the area. As we finished, we would lift the cross up and put it into the ground. As we slid the cross with Jesus on it into the ground, He asked for forgiveness for us. Why did we need forgiveness? Why didn't He hate us like every other condemned man? Didn't He realize that we were killing him?

133

Jesus on the cross

About three hours later, the entire land went dark. It was not like night. I just wanted this execution to be over. Then about three hours later, the darkness left, and I heard Jesus scream out, "My God, My God why have you forsaken me?" The cry was agonizing. It was the cry of a heartbreaking. I was thinking about this when He screamed out His final words. "It is finished."

I went up to the cross and asked a woman who this Jesus was. She broke down in tears and I couldn't understand her. But the man with her explained to me the story of Jesus. He tried to tell me that Jesus was the Messiah, but I wouldn't listen. Before I left, we went ahead and broke the legs of the other two criminals but didn't waste our time with Jesus. He was already dead. One of the soldiers ran a sword through His side.

The next week while going through the town, I saw a person who was the spitting image of Jesus. I could see the nail marks still in His wrists. As I stood there staring, He called to me and said, "I Am He." He had read my mind. I bowed down. He raised my head and told me, "What I had completely finished was paying for your sins. Go and sin no more, you are a new creation." Now as I go everywhere, I hear 'It is finished.' It is God's way of reminding me that sin is no longer my master."

—Alan G. Smith,
"Ramblings of a Roman Soldier"[2]

"Greater love has no one than this, to lay down one's life for his friends."

—John 15:13

I hope that this story of Jesus's last day will always be a reminder as to the ultimate sacrifice He made for every human being. He gave His life so that we sinners could be saved. It is through His suffering and death that we now have a pathway to eternal salvation.

At the beginning and the end of each day, we should humbly express our gratitude to Him by saying "Thank you, Jesus." And if we were to ask Him what He wants us to do, I trust the answer would be:

"Believe in me,

for I am the Way."

---

[1] Merton, Thomas, *Thoughts in Solitude.* Farrar, Straus and Giroux, 1999.

[2] *Inspirational Christian Stories and Poems (blog);* "Ramblings of a Roman Soldier," by Alan G. Smith, posted August 24, 2011.

About the Author

Richard DeGiacomo served as a United States Marine and is a veteran of the Korean War. After his service, he then attended at Boston College, where he graduated with a bachelor's degree in economics. He has had an extensive business career, and for the last thirteen years, he has been serving as a prison minister.

Richard has been married for sixty-two years to his wife, Elaine; and he has three children, six grandchildren, and four great-grandchildren.

If you'd like to contact Richard, email him at achristianlife3@gmail.com.

Other Books by Richard

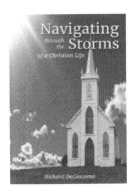

Navigating through the Storms of a Christian Life takes us on a journey through time and answers many of the questions we might have about our relationship with Jesus. It helps us understand who He is, why He came, what He did, and why He sacrificed Himself for the forgiveness of our sins.

Navigating through the Storms also explains the true meaning of Christianity and how its influence will help us get through the difficulties of this life and earn our reward of eternal salvation. Living a Christian life might at times not seem so easy; that could be so, but the reward sure is worth it.

Made in the USA
Columbia, SC
12 September 2021

44525659R00083